Black Holes

Contents

Written by Anna Claybourne

Collins

Dark stars

When telescopes were invented in 1609, scientists pointed
them at the sky and began to find out much more about space.
Italian scientist Galileo used an early telescope to see
Saturn's rings and Jupiter's moons, and he discovered
that the Milky Way was made of
billions of stars.

In 1784, a scientist called John Michell wrote about strange objects in space that swallowed light. He said that you could not see these objects, but he knew that they could make other stars move in a strange way. He called these objects "dark stars", but it was not until the 20th century that scientists found signs that dark stars really do exist. Today, we call them black holes.

What are black holes?

Black holes aren't actually holes. They don't lead anywhere – you can't go through a black hole and end up somewhere else.

A black hole is more like a tiny, invisible point in space, which works like a powerful plughole. Objects that come close to a black hole get pulled towards it, then disappear into it – whether they're very small, like dust, or large, like rocks. Black holes can even swallow whole moons, planets and stars. If a spaceship flew too close to a black hole, it would get pulled in too. So would you, if you were floating past in a spacesuit.

Rocks, gas and dust can all get pulled into black holes.

4

Where do black holes come from?

Black holes are formed from some kinds of stars when they get old and die. Not all stars turn into black holes, only the biggest ones.

Stars don't last forever. After burning for billions of years, they get old and begin to run out of fuel. It still takes a long time for a star to die – it can be millions of years. First, the star swells up and turns red. Most stars then shrink and cool down into a small, heavy ball of ash – a dead star. These dead stars are about the size of Earth, but much heavier – as heavy as the Sun.

How a dead star is formed

A star burns brightly for billions of years.

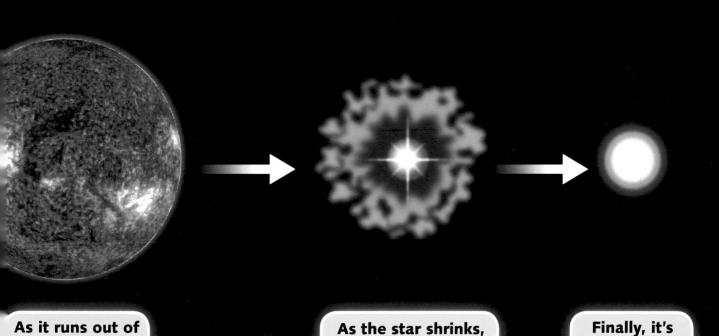

As it runs out of
fuel, it swells up
and turns red.

As the star shrinks,
a cloud of gas forms.

Finally, it's
a tiny, heavy,
dead star.

7

When a really giant star starts to die, it doesn't just get bigger, it explodes. This massive explosion is called a supernova. It's very big and it only takes a couple of minutes.

How a black hole is formed

A giant star burns for billions of years.

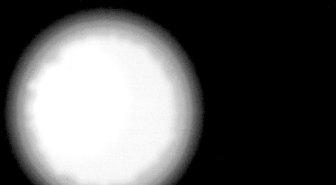

It swells up at the end of its life.

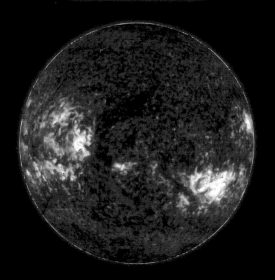

The star then collapses in on itself and shrinks to a tiny size. It becomes much smaller than a normal dead star. But as it has so much stuff crammed into it, it's also much, much heavier.

Finally, it becomes so tiny, it's just a very, very heavy dot in space. This is a black hole.

It can take a million years for a giant star to change and become a black hole at the end of its life.

A black hole is formed.

It explodes in a massive, bright supernova.

What do black holes do?

When an object gets close to a
black hole, it's pulled faster and
faster into the middle of it.
This happens because black holes
have very strong **gravity**.

Gravity is a pulling **force**. All objects
have it and the bigger the object,
the stronger its gravity. On Earth,
gravity is what makes an orange fall
when you throw it. It makes rivers
flow downhill and skateboarders
zoom down a ramp. Gravity holds
each person in place on the ground.
Without gravity, we'd float off
into space.

When you're on a slope, the pulling force of gravity drags you towards the bottom. If you're on wheels, or the surface is slippery, you zoom downhill.

When the gravity in a black hole pulls on objects, it doesn't just move them towards the middle of the black hole. It's so strong, and pulls so hard, it changes their shape.

The gravity in a black hole stretches and squishes objects as they get sucked in, making them longer and thinner. In the middle of the black hole, gravity **compresses** them so tightly, they get crushed down to nothing. If you looked inside a black hole you wouldn't see suns and moons floating about inside it – they have been crushed so small, you wouldn't see anything at all.

An object before it reaches a black hole.

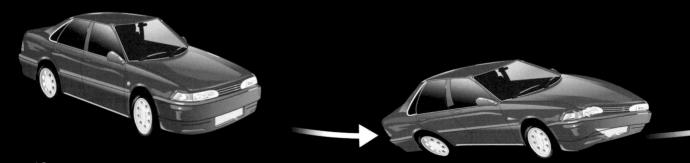

The object is pulled and crushed as it gets closer to the black hole.

13

Black holes are small but dense

All the stuff that gets sucked into a black hole is compressed into a tiny dot in the middle. That dot is smaller than a grape. It's smaller than a grain of sand. In fact, it's so small it takes up no space at all!

All the matter in a black hole takes up less space than a grain of sand.

If you could hold a black hole in your hand, it would be invisible, yet heavier than the Sun. The Sun weighs about 2,000,000,000,000,000,000,000,000,000,000 kilograms. That's 300,000 times more than Earth and 30 billion times more than you!

So how can something so small have such strong gravity? Black holes have strong gravity because they're very dense. Density means how heavy something is for its size.

A piece of packaging foam is very light. But a piece of gold exactly the same size is very heavy. This is because gold is denser than foam. It has more stuff packed into the same amount of space.

A piece of packaging foam is very light.

A piece of gold is much heavier than packaging foam.

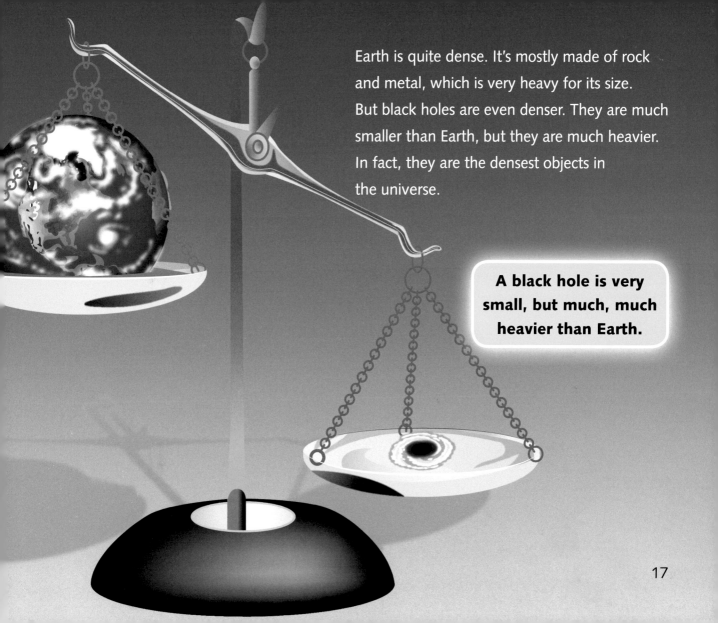

Earth is quite dense. It's mostly made of rock and metal, which is very heavy for its size. But black holes are even denser. They are much smaller than Earth, but they are much heavier. In fact, they are the densest objects in the universe.

A black hole is very small, but much, much heavier than Earth.

How do you find a black hole?

Space scientists look for black holes using telescopes. But how do you find something so tiny and invisible in space? Each black hole has a ball-shaped area around it. Within the ball-shaped area, nothing can escape from its gravity. This area is much bigger than the black hole itself.

Once something has passed into the ball-shaped area around a black hole, it can't be seen. But space scientists can see objects such as stars **orbiting** around the ball-shaped area and changing shape as they are pulled towards the black hole. The black hole's powerful gravity makes stars stretch out into a string, like a lump of modelling clay when you pull on it.

Objects are pulled towards the black hole.

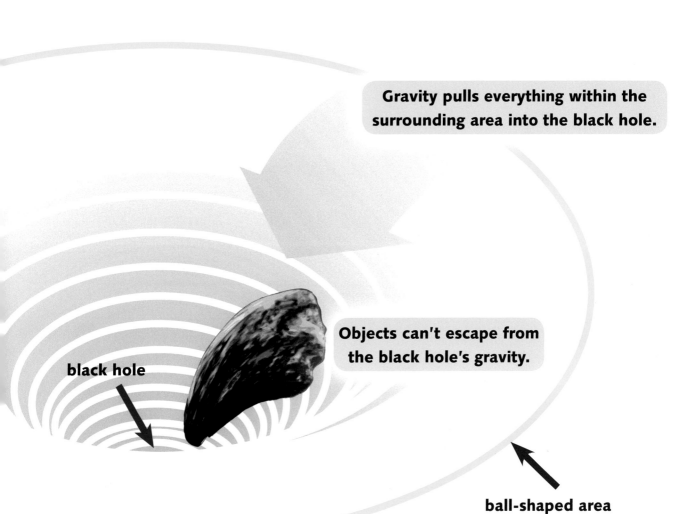

Gravity pulls everything within the surrounding area into the black hole.

Objects can't escape from the black hole's gravity.

black hole

ball-shaped area

As objects pass close to a black hole, its gravity may make them change direction. If they get close enough, they spiral around the black hole as they get sucked in, like water swirling down a plughole. The objects move faster and faster as they get closer to the middle. When space scientists see this "plughole effect" happening in space, it means they may have found a black hole.

If you half-fill a sink with water, add glitter to the water and then pull the plug out, the glitter will spiral around the plughole, going faster and faster as it gets closer to the middle. A black hole works the same way.

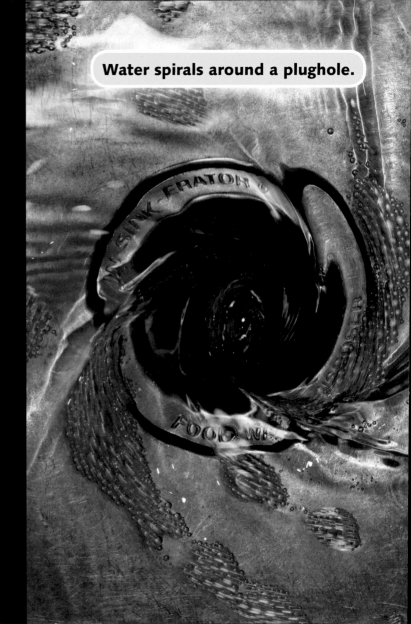

Water spirals around a plughole.

Space dust spirals around a black hole before getting sucked in.

Sometimes, a star is near a black hole, but not close enough to get sucked in. The black hole and the star pull on each other and orbit around each other. So if a space scientist sees a star circling around something they can't see, this can tell them where a black hole is hiding.

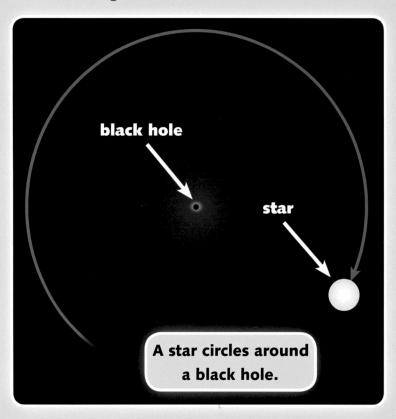

black hole

star

A star circles around a black hole.

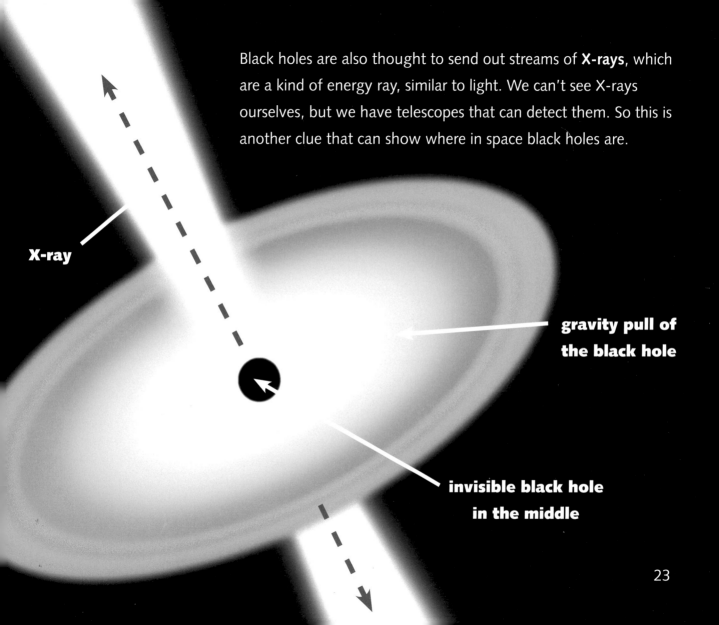

Black holes are also thought to send out streams of **X-rays**, which are a kind of energy ray, similar to light. We can't see X-rays ourselves, but we have telescopes that can detect them. So this is another clue that can show where in space black holes are.

X-ray

gravity pull of
the black hole

invisible black hole
in the middle

Naming black holes

When space scientists find something that looks like a black hole, they mark it on a map of the sky and give it a name. These names are made up of letters and numbers, which tell other space scientists where the black hole can be found.

Black holes are often named after the **constellations**, or star patterns, that are close to them in the sky. For example, there is a black hole among the stars of Cygnus, the swan. This black hole has been named Cygnus X-1.

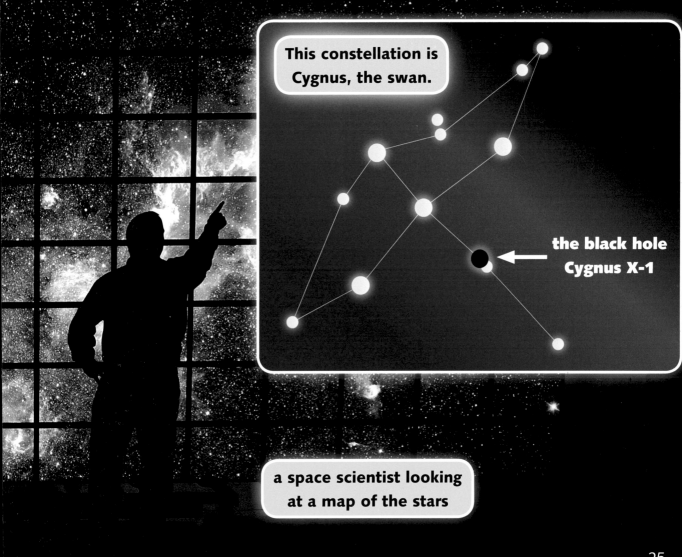

This constellation is Cygnus, the swan.

the black hole Cygnus X-1

a space scientist looking at a map of the stars

What does a black hole look like?

Black holes look black! Because they suck everything deep inside them, including light, they appear from the outside as nothing but darkness.

Space scientists are now hoping to take a real, close-up photograph of a black hole to see if it really does appear as a dark, round empty space. This has never been done before, as our telescopes have not been powerful enough. Space scientists plan to do it by combining the power of several different telescopes.

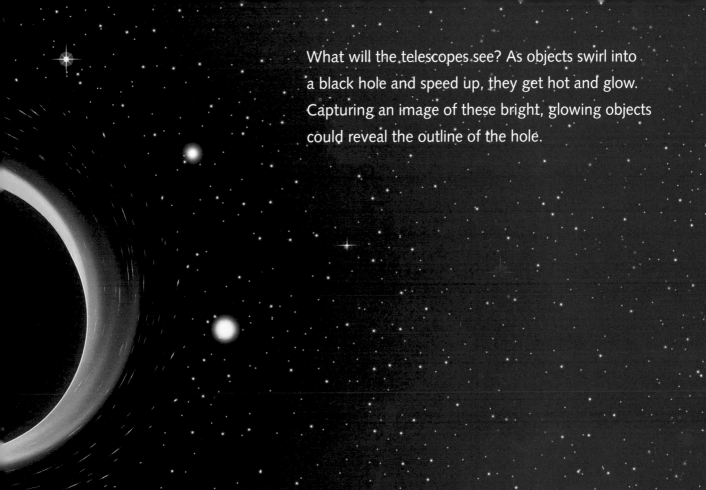

What will the telescopes see? As objects swirl into
a black hole and speed up, they get hot and glow.
Capturing an image of these bright, glowing objects
could reveal the outline of the hole.

27

What space scientists can tell us is that there are different kinds of black hole.

The simplest type of black hole is medium-sized and formed from a dead star.

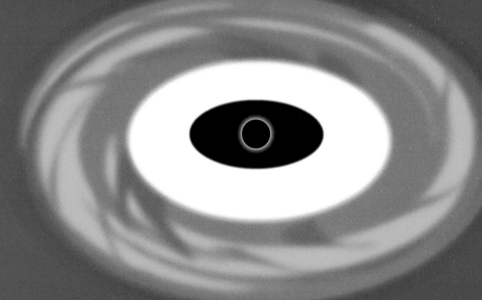

a simple black hole

Some black holes also rotate, or spin around.

Stars form from gas clumping together. As the gas gathers into a ball, its movement makes the star spin around. If a star comes close to another space object, it may get caught by its gravity and begin orbiting around it. Then, if a star becomes a black hole, this spinning or circling movement continues.

Some black holes seem to be much bigger than normal. Scientists are not sure how they formed.

a spinning black hole

Supermassive black holes

The biggest black holes of all are called "supermassive black holes". These are incredibly large, powerful black holes. A normal black hole might be around ten times as heavy as our Sun. A supermassive black hole could be millions, or even billions, of times heavier than our Sun.

No one is sure how supermassive black holes were made. They could have been normal black holes that just grew bigger and bigger.

Scientists think there is a supermassive black hole in the middle of our **galaxy**, the Milky Way.

Milky Way galaxy

Our Sun, solar system and Earth are here.

There may be a supermassive black hole here.

Our nearest black hole

Space scientists have now found lots of space objects that may be black holes. But even the nearest black holes to Earth can't be seen because they are still very, very far away. The fastest spaceship would have to fly for 17 million years to reach one!

One of the closest black holes to Earth is called A0620-00.

Although you can't see the black hole itself, if you live near the **equator** you can see a group of stars in the sky in the shape of a unicorn called Monoceros. That's where the black hole is. It may be the nearest black hole to Earth, but it's still over 30,000,000,000,000,000 kilometres away!

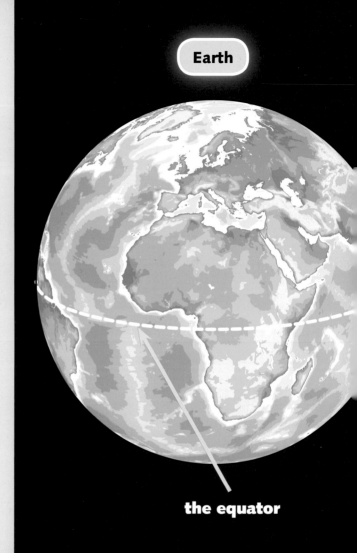

Earth

the equator

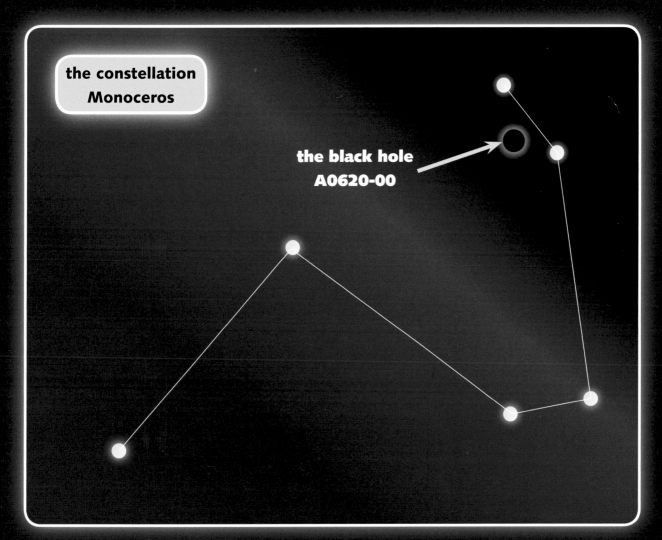

the constellation Monoceros

the black hole
A0620-00

Will Earth get sucked into a black hole?

Earth is so far away from the nearest black hole that its gravity isn't strong enough to pull us towards it at this distance. The farther away you are from something, the weaker its gravity feels. In this way, a black hole is just like Earth or the Sun. Their gravity only pulls in things that are close enough and a black hole is the same. We are nowhere near a black hole, so we aren't about to get sucked in.

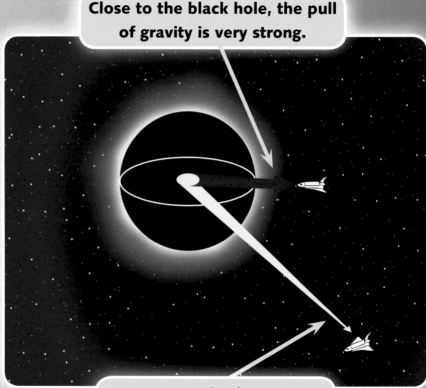

Close to the black hole, the pull of gravity is very strong.

As you get further away, the pull of gravity is weaker.

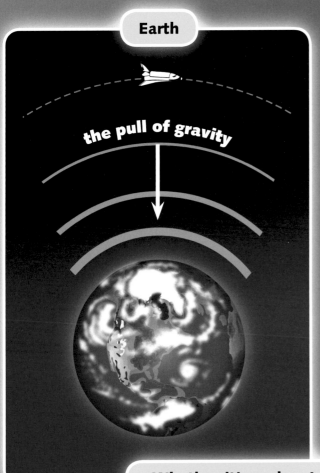

Earth

the pull of gravity

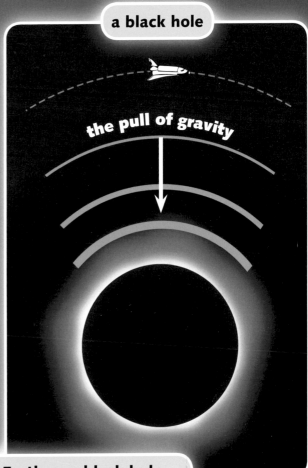

a black hole

the pull of gravity

Whether it's a planet like Earth or a black hole,
if you're far enough away gravity can't pull you in.

Beyond our galaxy

Besides studying black holes in our own galaxy, the Milky Way, space scientists are studying black holes in other galaxies. It was only in the 1920s, less than 100 years ago, that galaxies beyond our own were discovered. They are incredibly far away. But we now have telescopes that can spot signs of black holes there, too.

Powerful telescopes like these can detect distant galaxies.

Many galaxies, like ours, are a huge, whirling spiral shape. Scientists think all these galaxies probably have supermassive black holes in the middle. They have even spotted black holes swallowing other black holes.

some of the distant galaxies we've discovered

Searching the skies

From Earth

Space scientists use different types of telescopes to study the sky and search for black holes. But where's the best place to put a telescope?

To see space clearly, telescopes have to be far away from city lights. Too much light can get in the way of the faint glow from distant space objects. Air pollution and rain clouds also cause problems. So telescopes are often on top of high mountains or in deserts, where the sky is very clear.

Space scientists are working on a new, super-powerful telescope, which will help us see black holes. It will be made up of thousands of radio telescope dishes working together. They collect **radio waves** coming from faraway objects in space and turn them into images we can see.

a space **observatory** on top of Mauna Kea, a huge mountain in Hawaii

39

To get an even better view of space, some telescopes are in orbit around Earth. From there, they can view faraway space objects with no air, clouds or lights nearby.

They transmit images of space back to scientists on Earth in the form of radio messages. The Hubble Space Telescope is the most famous of all. It has been searching space for over 20 years, and has found black holes in distant galaxies.

the Hubble Space Telescope

As the Hubble telescope is getting quite old, a new, even better telescope is being built to replace it, called the James Webb Space Telescope. It will orbit much further out in space than Hubble. Space scientists hope it will tell us much more about black holes.

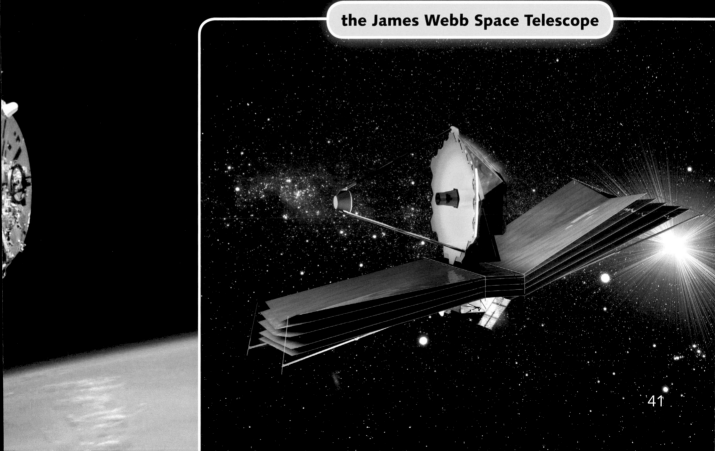

the James Webb Space Telescope

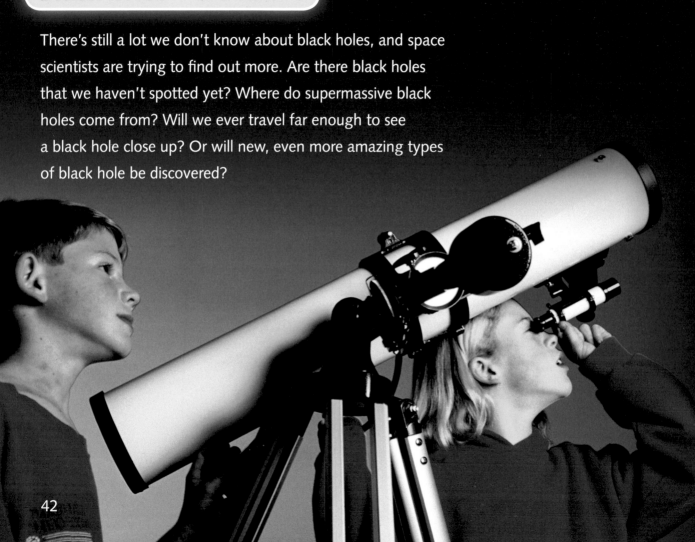

Black holes – the future

There's still a lot we don't know about black holes, and space scientists are trying to find out more. Are there black holes that we haven't spotted yet? Where do supermassive black holes come from? Will we ever travel far enough to see a black hole close up? Or will new, even more amazing types of black hole be discovered?

We've found out a huge amount about black holes since John Michell first wrote about them, more than 200 years ago. What might the next 200 years reveal?

an astronaut working in space

Glossary

compresses   squashes into a smaller space

constellations   groups of stars that seem to form a pattern in the sky

equator   an imaginary circle around the middle of Earth which divides the north and south of the planet and is the same distance from the north and south poles

force   a push or pull that can make something move or change

galaxy   a huge cluster of stars

gravity   a pulling force that comes from objects

observatory   a building used for viewing space

orbiting   circling around another object

radio waves   energy waves that are similar to light

X-rays   energy rays that are similar to light but invisible

Index

From star to black hole

a star

a star running out of fuel

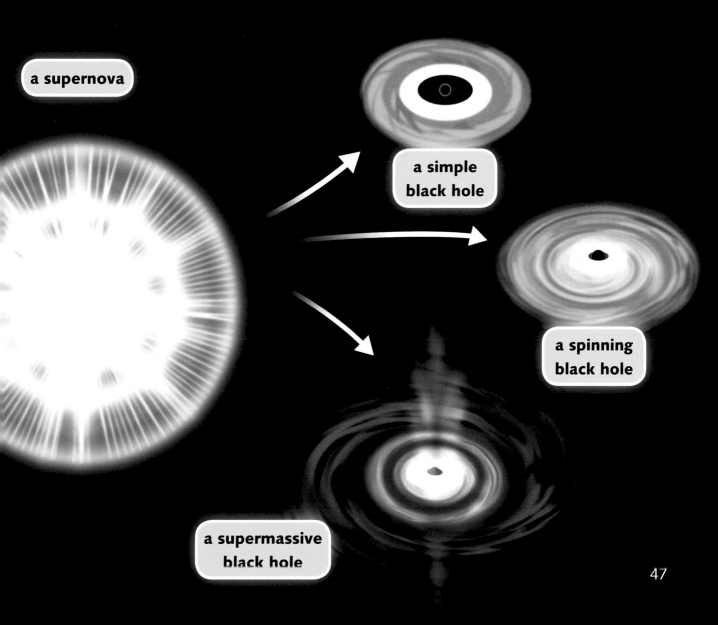

a supernova

a simple
black hole

a spinning
black hole

a supermassive
black hole

47

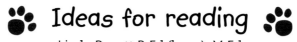 Ideas for reading

Linda Pagett B.Ed (hons), M.Ed
Lecturer and Educational Consultant

Learning objectives: develop a range of personal strategies for learning new words; identify and summarise evidence from a text to support a hypothesis; interrogate texts to deepen and clarify understanding and response; respond appropriately to the contributions of others; listen to a speaker

Curriculum links: Science

Interest words: black holes, compresses, constellation, equator, galaxy, gravity, Jupiter, Milky Way, orbiting, radio waves, rotate, Saturn, supernova, telescope, X-rays

Resources: black paper, white pens

Getting started

This book can be read over two or more reading sessions.

- Explain that this is a book about the universe. Discuss what children already know about space, e.g. the names of planets in our system.

- Invite one of the children to read the blurb. Has anyone heard of black holes before? As a group, predict what black holes might be.

- Discuss the words in the glossary and ensure children understand their meanings.

- Remind children of strategies for reading tricky words, e.g. sounding out or guessing from surrounding text.

Reading and responding

- Ask children to read silently to p9 and check they have understood what black holes are and how they are made.

- Encourage them to make notes and write down any questions they have or areas they are unsure of, but explain that these notes must be very short and that they may use pictures and diagrams as references.

- Ask children to read to p43, supporting weaker readers by prompting and praising.